Cottagecore

New Countryside Living

gestalten

Contents

Slow Living

How Rural Spaces Are Reframing Contemporary Living

The alarm sounds at 06:30 in a studio overlooking concrete and steel. The commute looms ahead with its cramped subway cars; later, one looks forward to fluorescent office lights, and the relentless ping of notifications. By evening, the city dweller is drained by the very energy that once made life there so intoxicating. This is often the modern urban experience: a life of stimulation that has become disorienting, a fast-paced existence that leaves little room for the slow rhythms that ground us.

Yet, a subtle revolution has taken root: urbanites are stepping away from metropolises, trading cramped apartments for rural cottages, frantic schedules for seasonal rhythms, and digital saturation for the tactile pleasure of tending gardens and lighting wood stoves. And many aren't fleeing to pristine suburban developments, but rather to modest homes with crooked doorframes and uneven floors—spaces that require patience, creativity, and a willingness to work with what exists rather than tear it down.

This movement, which found its voice in the cottagecore aesthetic that captured imaginations across social media starting in 2018, represents something deeper than a trend. It reflects a shift in how we understand home, community, and the good life. Born of a millennial disillusionment with the promises of urban success, cottagecore began as an internet phenomenon celebrating pastoral simplicity, handmade crafts, and the romance of rural living. But what started as a series of Instagram posts has evolved into a genuine lifestyle movement.

Above Maison Hécourt in France showcases wooden beams and a stone exterior that honor traditional craftsmanship, yet remains decidedly modern in its approach—embodying the cottagecore movement's maturation beyond nostalgic imitation toward spaces that engage authentically with place and history.

This ethos extends beyond the act of simply relocating to the countryside. The cottagecore mindset—embracing imperfection, celebrating handmade objects, finding beauty in mismatched elements, and prioritizing authenticity over aspiration—can flourish anywhere. Urban dwellers are discovering that thrifting furniture instead of buying new, learning to repair rather than replace, and creating homes that reflect personal histories can transform even the smallest spaces into sanctuaries.

Cottagecore reflects a shift in how we understand home, community, and the good life and has evolved into a genuine lifestyle movement.

The properties featured here tell the story of that evolution across continents—from the Scottish Highlands to rural Australia, from the forests of Germany to the countryside of Massachusetts and beyond. They belong to homeowners who've discovered that good design doesn't require unlimited budgets or exacting aesthetics. Instead, these spaces reveal how creativity flourishes within constraints, how character emerges from imperfection, and how the most meaningful interiors are shaped by the daily rituals of their inhabitants.

These are not the pristine country homes of shelter magazines, where every surface gleams and every corner is styled for the camera. They're lived-in spaces that bear the marks of life—children's toys scattered across salvaged-wood floors, walls painted in bold colors that shift with seasonal light, or kitchens where ceramic vessels hold wildflowers gathered during morning walks. They represent a rejection of the disposable culture that dominates contemporary living, embracing instead the beauty of patina and the wisdom of making do with what you have and making it beautiful in the process.

Cottagecore living speaks to broader cultural anxieties about sustainability, authenticity, and the pace of modern life. In an era of climate crisis and social isolation, these homes offer a different model that prioritizes connection over consumption, craftsmanship over convenience. They demonstrate how

design-literate urbanites can adapt to rural contexts without imposing urban values.

This movement isn't without its complexities, of course. The rural sensibility shaped by urban migrants raises questions about gentrification, affordability, and the displacement of locals. The romance of country living often obscures the economic realities that drive people from cities: rising rents, stagnant wages, and the impossibility of homeownership. What appears as a lifestyle choice is frequently born of necessity.

These homes represent a rejection of the disposable culture, embracing instead the wisdom of making do with what you have and making it beautiful in the process.

This collection navigates these tensions with honesty and grace, showing how thoughtful design can emerge from limited budgets: antique dealers transforming rural properties through thoughtful curation, former restaurant chefs building gathering spaces around the idea of hospitality, and artists who understand that rebellion can sometimes be disguised as domesticity. These spaces also prove that materiality matters, that the texture of aged wood, the weight of handmade ceramics, and the warmth of natural light create atmospheres that can't be easily duplicated.

This book arrives at a moment when the cottagecore movement has matured beyond its Instagram origins to become a legitimate alternative to urban living. As remote work normalizes and housing costs push more and more people out of cities, these homes are increasingly relevant. They offer a blueprint for living that's both economically sustainable and emotionally nourishing.

In a world increasingly dominated by the virtual, these properties assert the importance of the physical—spaces that can be touched, smelled, and inhabited. They remind us that home is not only shelter but sanctuary, no mere backdrop but rather a stage for living well. They show that the antidote to urban burnout isn't escape, but a deeper engagement with place and history via spaces that serve the lives lived within them.

Tivoli, New York, USA
by Ghislaine Viñas

The Imperfectionists

When Ghislaine and Jaime Viñas found a sign in the attic reading "This is it!" they took it as divine intervention. Their neglected Arts and Crafts cottage in Tivoli was destined for demolition until that discovery changed everything. What followed was a renovation philosophy that treats imperfection as inheritance: doors scratched by pets painted over in saturated green, original millwork preserved despite its quirks, and a river-rock chimney painted white to highlight rather than conceal its texture.

Known for her bold commercial interiors, Ghislaine brings that same fearlessness to rural domesticity. Her custom "Mad Plaider" wallpaper wraps the living room in deep green, while an egg-yolk-yellow front door announces her design manifesto: make people smile. The interiors feel curated rather than decorated, replete with Pakistani artwork, Hudson Valley birdhouses, and a vibrant patchwork of flea-market finds.

This is cottagecore with an urban sensibility: Ghislaine spends half her time in the city, bringing metropolitan confidence to the 46 acres (18.6 hectares) of this Catskill landscape. Enlarged kitchen windows frame morning coffee rituals with views of wildlife, while newly mowed paths through fields become spaces for meditation. The couple's integration into the local creative community reflects a broader shift in rural living, where country homes serve as cultural bridges rather than escapes.

This is a renovation as an intimate autobiography, where every preserved flaw and bold gesture writes another chapter in a home's ongoing story.

Opposite Designer Ghislaine Viñas covered the walls of the living room in her signature "Mad Plaider" wallpaper in a vibrant shade of green.
Above The kitchen windows were enlarged to maximize natural light and views of the surrounding nature.

Opposite A mixture of flea market finds, artworks, and accessories bring a lived-in, curated sensibility to the rooms.
Above Bold touches of color, from painted walls to unusual design pieces and art, infuse the historic home with a playful, contemporary feel.

Bozen's Cottage

Oatlands, Tasmania, Australia
by Taylor + Hinds Architects

Time as Material

In a Tasmanian townscape where Georgian buildings quietly bear witness to Australia's colonial history, Bozen's Cottage displays a nuanced approach to preservation, one that honors both architectural heritage and the rhythms of continuous habitation. Named for its previous owner, whose family occupied the 1842 sandstone dwelling for over a century, the four-room structure had reached a critical point of deterioration when its new owner intervened in 2017.

Poppy Taylor and Mat Hinds's method feels almost archaeological. Instead of imposing contemporary ideals, they engaged in "adaptive repair," guided by the raw qualities of Vandemonian Georgian architecture: economy, material honesty, and an undercurrent of isolation shaped by landscape. J. C. Loudon's *An Encyclopedia of Cottage, Farm, and Villa Architecture and Furniture* (1833) also served as a reference, allowing interventions to converse with the home's primitive mannerisms rather than overwrite them.

Where fire once scarred the northeastern elevation, two large windows now gather morning light and frame the gardens. Finely crafted insertions pay homage to generations of blacksmiths, carpenters, and pastoralists: window seats nestled into thick stone walls, or wooden shutters that provide tactile engagement with both material and memory.

A small enclosed porch at the rear opens to a courtyard, where salvaged brick fills an "archaeological" field of foundations, stoops, and hearths—a careful layering that lets past and present coexist, and invites a slower, more attentive way of dwelling.

Above Originally built in 1842, the typical Tasmanian-Georgian cottage still bears marks of its past, including hand-hewn sandstone and brick.
Opposite Original pit-sawn boards and salvaged woodwork stand as living witnesses to two centuries of craft and care.

Above From the interiors to the exterior, Georgian restraint meets delicate contemporary insertions, weaving a layered narrative of stewardship, memory, and respectful renewal.
Opposite Morning light spills across a hand-stitched quilt, echoing the cottage's long lineage of care and domestic ritual.

Nieby, Schleswig-Holstein, Germany
by Jan Henrik Jansen and Marshall Blecher

A Respectful Revival

In an age obsessed with newness, there's a particular wisdom in knowing when to hold back. On Germany's Baltic coast, Jan Henrik Jansen and Marshall Blecher resurrected a 120-year-old crofter's cottage into something that defies easy categorization—neither strictly traditional nor contemporary, but rather something deeply nuanced.

The dwelling's modesty belies its history. Built by farmers in the late 1800s, the thatch-roofed, brick structure had suffered from collapsed ceilings, an awkwardly appended pigsty, and partial roof failure. Its transformation speaks to architecture's potential not just to preserve, but to reinterpret with restraint.

The street-facing facade remains deliberately untouched—a quiet acknowledgment of regional vernacular. Around the building, a contemporary sensibility gradually emerges, with a black-steel dormer window offering the first clue that something more substantial has occurred.

The interior's spatial reconsideration is perhaps the property's most profound. Where 14 cramped rooms once created a domestic labyrinth, a single kitchen and dining space anchored by a concrete plinth now stands. Throughout, textures of past and present are in dialogue: chamois-plastered walls against precisely crafted German oak woodwork, and exposed historic rafters alongside triple-glazed windows. The rear opens to a private yard through windows cut into previously damaged brick.

For its Hamburg-based owners (weekenders for now), the cottage represents a domestic evolution: not a rejection of modernity but a reconsideration of what connects a space to both place and purpose.

Opposite Surrounded by fields of barley, the cottage was originally built by tenant farmers—also known as crofters—in the late 1800s. *Above* Though the home still holds suggestions of its historic past, such as the thatched roof, the interior is thoroughly contemporary.

Above A black steel dormer window, exposed oak rafters, and textured chamois plaster walls were all incorporated into the thoughtful restoration. *Opposite* In an area where many similar buildings were revived beyond recognition, it was important for the architects and owners to maintain the exterior's historic appearance.

TILL KARIN
AUG. 1894

The Original Cottage Rebels

How a Swedish artistic couple understood the radical power inherent in domestic spaces long before cottagecore became a trend.

The Larssons' legacy anticipates our cottagecore moment: the recognition that domestic rebellion remains one of the most radical acts available to us.

Carl and Karin Larsson's transformation of Lilla Hyttnäs, a modest log cottage in Sundborn, north of Stockholm, wasn't mere home improvement; it was cultural insurgency disguised as domesticity. By rejecting the oppressive formality of 19th-century Swedish bourgeois life, they created something revolutionary: a house that dared to be joyful. In 1888, when Karin's father gifted the couple this remote cottage, Sweden's upper classes were trapped in the German Lutheran–influenced academic style—imposing, dark-brown antique furnishings and excessive neo-Renaissance ornamentation. The Larssons saw this aesthetic prison and chose something else. Over three decades, they transformed their home into an elaborate meta-art project, a hand-embellished 14-room sanctuary that would fundamentally challenge how domestic spaces function and feel.

What makes Lilla Hyttnäs significant isn't just its influence on Nordic design (though that's undeniable), but how it anticipated our contemporary hunger for homes that feel authentic rather than aspirational. The Larssons painted over antique furniture with a cheerful disregard for provenance, mixed high and low materials, and let their children's faces float like cherubic graffiti across walls and doors.

Influenced by William Morris and John Ruskin, who preached the democratization of design and the merits of craftsmanship over mass production, the couple entirely rejected traditional spatial hierarchies. There would be no central parlor for entertaining, no grand entrance or servants' wings. Instead, narrow corridors hung with gallery-style drawings led to lofty expanses and clusters of jewel-box rooms. The dining room epitomized their aesthetic rebellion: intense tomato-red and forest-green hues, cheap reed-and-bead paneling typically relegated to kitchens, and Karin's "Four Elements" tapestry with plum, royal blue, and tangerine colliding with Modernist geometric forms.

Above The exterior of Lilla Hyttnäs shows the traditional red-painted wooden cottage set in the picturesque village of Sundborn, Sweden. *Opposite* The decor bursts with vibrant patterns and colors, transforming this room that was once Carl's painting studio into a celebration of the couple's rejection of formal Victorian interiors.

Above A hallway where traditional Swedish wood paneling and folk-inspired paintings merge with modern and whimsical touches.
Opposite A cozy seating area featuring walls covered in Carl's paintings—including *The Riddle of Life* (1911) depicting children posing with a skull—and a long red bench demonstrate the couple's masterful juxtaposition of color and patterns.

The couple's approach feels surprisingly modern. They prioritized experience over hierarchy, choosing materials for joy rather than status. Karin's sophisticated folk-art sensibility—sunflower-tentacled cushions and hieroglyphic table runners—created a visual language that celebrated the everyday while maintaining artistic rigor.

Carl's watercolor documentation of their life, published in *Ett hem* (A Home, 1899) and *Das Haus in der Sonne* (The House in the Sun, 1909), didn't just capture their domestic experiment; it exported a new vision of rural Nordic wholesomeness that helped shape Sweden's national identity. Their influence extends far beyond Scandinavia, inspiring everything from Marimekko's bold patterns to Charleston's painted hearths.

The Larssons understood that true luxury lies not in expensive materials or formal grandeur, but in spaces that nurture creativity, celebrate family, and honor the transformative power of making things by hand. Their legacy anticipates our cottagecore moment: the recognition that domestic rebellion—choosing joy over status, handmade over mass-produced, authentic over aspirational—remains one of the most radical acts available to us.

Right The main entrance, painted in the signature red and green palette, with ivy growing up the exterior walls. The cottage represents classic Swedish timber architecture—a traditional log house built in 1837, featuring horizontally laid logs interlocked at the corners, a construction method that dominated Swedish residential building for centuries due to the country's abundant woodlands.

Brookside Cottage

Buckland, Gloucestershire,
United Kingdom

Where Time Deepens

In Buckland village, home to some 200 residents, Brookside Cottage stands as a counterargument to a contemporary rural development marked by expansion and modernization. Instead, this 15th-century limestone dwelling demonstrates how preservation can engender liberation rather than limitation, with historic constraints creating the character modern homes often lack.

The cottage's traditional Cotswold vocabulary—dormer and mullion windows, inglenook fireplaces, deep limestone walls—speaks to an architectural approach that has evolved through centuries of lived experience. The undulating oak floorboards upstairs reveal a building that has settled into itself. Whereas contemporary renovations might rush to level such imperfections, here they're testaments to the home's ongoing dialogue with its inhabitants. This relationship between dwelling and dweller also manifests in the gardens, defined by a series of individual spaces rather than manicured landscapes.

For today's residents, life at Brookside offers a remarkable shift from urban expectations. The village's lack of a through road ensures calm, while the neighboring church tower marks time visually rather than audibly. Even the owners' preference for entering through the rear stone terrace demonstrates the way in which historical spaces encourage personalization.

This is countryside living offering not so much an escape from modernity but a reconnection with the rhythms that predate it.

Opposite Boasting stone walls and surrounded by gardens and a brook, the 15th-century cottage embodies idyllic Cotswolds charm. Inside, an open-tread staircase leads to a generous upstairs landing that houses bedrooms.
Above Found at the front of the house, the dining area's cozy sensibility is enhanced by a stone hearth and an Esse Ironheart wood-burning stove.

Above Beautiful wallpaper adorns the walls of one of the three bedrooms upstairs.
Opposite Above a generous double butler's sink, stone mullion windows look out onto the rear garden from the kitchen.
Floral wallpaper and a classic stone hearth lend the main bedroom both elegance and character.

2019
SUN
15
September

KRAKEN

The Lizard, Cornwall,
United Kingdom

At the Sea's Edge

Above Interiors, as seen in this bedroom and living space, hint at the rural coastal location, with a neutral palette of whites and beige accented by seaside elements, including nautical stripes, a life ring, and artworks showcasing maritime themes that pay tribute to the building's seafaring past.
Opposite The maritime home features a generous rooftop terrace that nods to its historic use as a signal beacon for sailors navigating one of Cornwall's most rugged and treacherous stretches of coastline along the wild Lizard Peninsula.

Perched atop Cornwall's wild and windswept Lizard Peninsula, the Signal Station is an architectural ode to life at the edge of the world. Once a beacon guiding mariners to safety, the historic 1872 structure has been reborn as the ultimate coastal sanctuary—an embodiment of a yearning for simpler, nature-immersed living. Inside, the interiors exude understated maritime elegance: whitewashed wooden walls, soft hues of blue and gray, and nautical stripes echo the sea beyond every window. Salvaged fittings and maritime maps pay tribute to the building's seafaring past, while window seats encourage long hours of tea-sipping, book-reading, or simply storm-watching as gulls fly past.

Each detail was designed to foster warmth and intimacy. There aren't any harsh overhead spotlights to disrupt the cozy glow, and cushions and blankets abound to create a sense of *hygge* in every nook. From the airy living spaces to the crow's nest bar that opens onto a panoramic roof terrace, every corner celebrates the untamed beauty of the surrounding landscape. Life here feels wonderfully slow: mornings spent stretching into the sunrise on the terrace, afternoons exploring rugged coves along the coastline, and evenings watching the sky set ablaze over the Atlantic. At the Signal Station, rural coastal living transcends escape. It becomes an invitation to reconnect with nature, embrace the elements, and savor the time-honored romance of the sea.

CAP WEST
10-88

Opposite A communal dining table with bench seating creates an intimate gathering space.
Above The dramatic clifftop location offers sweeping views from the rooftop terrace across one of Cornwall's most stunning seascapes.

Berkshires Farmhouse

Berkshires, Massachusetts, USA
by Lauren and Suzanne McGrath, McGrath II

Inherited Wisdom

Above In this cozy reading nook, weathered wooden beams reflect the historic integrity of the farmhouse, which dates back to 1764.
Opposite Throughout the ground floor, peach-hued plaster walls both soften and highlight the exposed-beam ceilings, lending the space an inviting, English cottage charm.

When a burst pipe forces your hand, you can either panic or pivot. Lauren and Suzanne McGrath chose the latter, transforming what could have been a restoration disaster into an opportunity for mindful intervention. This 1764 Berkshires farmhouse, a weekend retreat for city-dwelling clients, now bears the hallmarks of designers who understand that the best rural homes don't announce their improvements but allow the space to absorb them.

The McGraths' approach reads like a master class in restraint. Rather than overwhelming the low-ceilinged rooms with period pastiche, they enlisted a local plasterer to envelop the ground floor in soft, peach-hued walls that evoke the classic English cottage while remaining thoroughly contemporary. Exposed beams left deliberately weathered anchor rooms furnished with mid-century finds, and a farmhouse table complements a camelback sofa repurposed in a cheerful Robert Kime textile.

This is the kind of casual confidence that comes from trusting instincts over trends. A butter-yellow kitchen island provides a bold gesture, while reclaimed-wood flooring (sourced after the water damage caused by the burst pipe) now appears convincingly historic. The result is a home that feels both preserved and refreshed, where extended family gatherings flow naturally between the functional cook's kitchen and the dining room's working fireplace.

This is preservation without preciousness, where historical integrity serves contemporary comfort instead of constraining it.

Opposite Berkshires Farmhouse was conceived for relaxation but also for entertainment. The owners love cooking and often host gatherings at the dining room table. *Above* A mix of vintage pieces, upholstered seating, and objects embracing a rural cottage style contribute to the home's casual, comfortable feel.

Right A soaring ceiling, wooden beams, and generous windows that allow abundant light to flow in define this casual living room—the perfect space for the owners to unwind and relax.

Compton, Hampshire,
United Kingdom
by G. H. Kitchin

Architectural Heritage Meets Horticultural Splendor

Above Beams overhead and wooden floors underfoot reinforce the warm cottage aesthetic throughout the interiors.
Opposite Surrounded by an Arts and Crafts–style garden that's
remained essentially unchanged, the original thatched cottage dates to the 17th century.

Located just three miles (4.8 kilometers) from Winchester in Hampshire's countryside, Compton End is a home where each century has added to what has come before. This heritage-protected architectural treasure began its life as a modest, 17th-century thatched cottage before doubling in size in the 18th century. Winchester architect G. H. Kitchin gave the house its most distinctive character, transforming it between 1891 and 1920 into a countryside home that marries the vernacular with Arts and Crafts style.

Inside, various elements ground the home in its rural heritage. In the double reception room, a bressummer beam crowns the space, its dark hue finding a counterpart in the inglenook fireplace. The kitchen offers a continuation, with wooden floors and beams overhead.

Perhaps most enchanting is Kitchin's garden room, a sunny space that makes brilliant use of a slanted wall and a number of former shop windows. Recognized on England's Register of Parks and Gardens of Special Historic Interest, the gardens show Kitchin's knack for creating what H. Avray Tipping called a "tenderly cultured oasis." At the property's southern edge, a pink summerhouse boasts windows on all four sides, while a restored 17th-century barn now serves as a library and storage space.

Compton End achieves what many countryside homes aspire to but few accomplish: a sense that history isn't something to be kept behind glass, but lived day-to-day, with each generation participating in a continuing story.

Opposite Rooms layered with upholstered furniture, patterned textiles, and antiques exquisitely capture English country style.
Above Architect G. H. Kitchin effectively doubled the size of the home
in the late 19th and early 20th century, with his Arts and Crafts renovation respecting the vernacular.

Above From a pink summer house to wild gardens and interiors full of character, Compton End embodies the quintessence of rural English living.
Opposite A detail of the 17th-century exterior: the oak frame is filled with bricks and crowned with a thatched roof.

Les Goudes, Marseille, France

Refuge at the Edge of the World

When Paris-based couple Xavier and Pauline Favre acquired their barnacle-like *cabanon* in Les Goudes, they inherited both a modest retreat and a piece of Marseille's soul. This 1960s fisherman's perch, cantilevered over Mediterranean waters within the protected Calanques National Park, represents something increasingly rare: an authentic coastal refuge untouched by luxury development.

The *cabanon's* patchwork character—terra-cotta tiles, blue-painted wooden balconies, low ceilings—speaks to decades of pragmatic evolution under working-class stewardship. Rather than sanitize this heritage, the Favres embraced its eccentric framework while layering in references that blur cultural boundaries: its lime-washed paneling evokes Alpine chalets, just as the nautical palette echoes one of their favorite hotels, La Minervetta, in Sorrento, Italy.

Their approach to furnishing was equally inventive, with contemporary ceramics and paintings sourced from local Marseille shops owned by friends. This isn't curation as status performance but as community investment, supporting regional makers while building a collection rooted in place.

What emerges is neither nostalgic pastiche nor gentrified retreat, but something more honest: a space that honors its proletarian origins while accommodating the needs of a contemporary retreat. In an era of coastal commodification, the Favres' *cabanon* offers an inspired alternative, where authenticity isn't marketed but lived, and where proximity to urban culture doesn't preclude a sense of genuine escape.

Opposite The owners decided to embrace the cabin's existing eccentricity, as seen in this living room, where a low ceiling, lime-washed walls, and a nautical palette mix Alpine charm with coastal style.
Above The *cabanon*—with its red roof tiles and distinctive blue balcony—is situated right at the water's edge at the Rocher des Goudes.

This isn't curation as status performance but as community investment, supporting regional makers while building a collection rooted in place.

Above Pops of color—cement tiles in the kitchen, textiles in the bedroom—punctuate the otherwise lime-washed interior. *Opposite* Retro-style banquettes and a dining table enliven the small dining room of this restored 1960s fisherman's cottage.

From Flat White to Firewood

How a Generation Traded Urban Cool for Rural Calm.

A new rural rhythm emerged, with relaxed morning rituals replacing morning commutes, and gardens becoming both sanctuaries and sources of sustenance.

Where hipster culture celebrated the handmade as an aesthetic, cottagecore emphasizes the act itself. What began as curated urban cool (think third-wave coffee, reclaimed wood, and obscure vinyl) has morphed into something more subtle and more practical. The migration from Brooklyn to off-grid, upstate cabins isn't just a physical one; it marks a deeper cultural shift from performing authenticity to actually living it.

Defined by irony, subcultural fluency, and aesthetic maximalism, the hipster emerged in the early 2000s. Neighborhoods like Williamsburg in Brooklyn, Berlin's Kreuzberg, and Hackney in East London became ground zeroes for this nascent identity, complete with indie cafés, typewritten menus, and carefully curated heritage fashion. However, when its authenticity became commodified, contradictions emerged: when brunch costs $40 and rents are more expensive than mortgages, the romance of an urban refuge begins to sour.

With its prairie dresses, sourdough starters, and idyllic fields, cottagecore might seem like a mere social-media trend, but it also represents a post-hipster evolution. Where hipster culture admired the handmade from a distance, cottagecore finds meaning in the making—hands in dough, knees in the soil. Urbanites who once Instagrammed latte art now grow their own kale. The shift is more than just aesthetic. It's philosophical.

The Covid-19 pandemic accelerated this transition because it forced stillness, fueled burnout, and revealed how fragile modern life really is. The Great Resignation soon followed in 2021 and 2022, as many professionals reassessed their relationship to work, space, and time. Moving to the countryside wasn't just about affordability—it was also about autonomy. Why pay $3,000 a month for a cramped studio in Greenpoint when you could have a house, garden, and room to breathe?

Thus, a new rural rhythm emerged, with relaxed morning rituals replacing morning commutes, and gardens becoming both sanctuaries and sources

Opposite A thriving garden with protective fencing showcases the self-sufficiency that defines post-hipster rural living, where homesteading skills have replaced cultural capital as markers of authenticity.
Above A rural dweller stands confidently outside her front door, surrounded by the evidence of a life grounded in practical skills: timber frames, well-used tools, and a work apron that speaks to hands-on living.

Above Dining outdoors with sweeping views of rolling hills and water embodies the cottagecore philosophy of integrating daily rituals with nature's rhythms.
Opposite A cozy kitchen often serves as the heart of rural home life, where many cottagecore followers find fulfillment in cooking from scratch and sourcing their own ingredients.

of sustenance. Homes, then, are no longer polished photoshoot sets, but places shaped by use, complete with wood stoves, open shelving for preserves, frayed linen napkins, and baskets of kindling by the door. Style concerns itself less with novelty and more with continuity and care.

This shift also redefines cultural capital. Cultural capital has moved from insider knowledge to practical skills: from knowing the rarest vinyl pressings to knowing how to preserve peaches or rotate crops. Do you know how to compost, build a fence, or bake bread? The currency has changed from disposable income to disposable time, from consumption to creation.

On an emotional level, the tone has shifted, too. Urban hipsterism thrived on irony; cottagecore leans into earnestness. There's no wink when you're splitting firewood or learning to can tomatoes: these things are messy, real, and require full engagement. There's power in the kind of sincerity. These rituals reconnect us to time, seasons, and ultimately to our bodies, and they offer the kind of meaning no new fashion fad, trendy spot, or algorithm can provide.

Of course, the performance hasn't vanished. Instagram still buzzes with carefully styled images of rustic life. The vintage quilt and obligatory backyard chickens may be the new status symbols, but there's a big difference when aesthetics intersect with necessity. When your heat comes from the wood you chop, style has stakes.

Cottagecore isn't just a trend cycle; it's also a recalibration. Amid global instability, rising costs, and climate dread, the movement offers something tangible: interiors shaped with intention, routines grounded in the physical world, and homes that prioritize feeling over flashy accents. Cottagecore homes aren't idealized escapes. Rather, they're lived-in, layered, and beautifully imperfect. And with many former hipsters choosing to live slower, with more care and less noise, a new kind of cool emerges, less a rebellion against something than a return to roots.

Right A plush chair paired with an antique rug beside a working fireplace creates the perfect setting for the slower pace these homes are designed to nurture.

Schorfheide, Brandenburg, Germany
by Caroline Lossberg

The Honest House

There's a particular honesty to Caroline Lossberg's approach to this renovated barn in Schorfheide, north of Berlin. It's an admission that real life is messier than editorial spreads might suggest. "Most of the time, the place doesn't look as tidy and clean as in the pictures," she shares, describing floors as covered in toys and children who bring slugs indoors. This candor reveals something essential about contemporary rural living: it's not about achieving pristine domesticity so much as creating space for authentic life.

The barn's previous owner spent years sourcing historic windows and accessories, and Lossberg built upon this foundation with upcycled furniture and her grandmother's floral-carved cabinet, now filled with old porcelain. Her decision to paint every blank wall in subtle or bold colors transformed the space and helped define each room's character.

The space isn't Instagram-perfect but something more valuable: a home that shifts with the seasons. Summer doors left open blur the boundaries between interiors and the garden, whereas winters see gatherings around the fireplace after walks in the snow. The barn's history as a village kindergarten adds resonance: once again filled with children, it completes a generational circle.

Lossberg's pottery studio is tucked within the property, demonstrating how rural retreats can nurture personal creativity. The cottage reflects an expansion of possibility and is proof that the most meaningful luxury might simply be the time and space required to remember what is life-giving and essential.

Opposite Old and new upcycled furniture and decor comes together with historic beams and stone flooring in the living area.
Above Relaxing hues of forest green and soft blue from Farrow & Ball adorn stairs, cupboards, and walls.

Opposite A man from the local village told the cottage's current owner that the structure once housed a kindergarten.
Above The owners, a couple and their children from Berlin, envisioned the cottage as a place where they could all reset and reconnect with nature.

Contemporary rural living is not about achieving pristine domesticity so much as creating space for authentic life.

Above From soft textiles to natural materials, every corner of this home embraces an atmosphere of peace and calm.
Opposite A child's bedroom. The owners intended for the home to be a comfortable, fluid space where their children could freely roam.

Accord, New York, USA
by Keren Craig and Piers North

A Patient Transformation

When Keren Craig and Piers North acquired this Hudson Valley barn, they embarked on what would become a 14-year master class in artful transformation. Rather than rush toward completion, they allowed the project to evolve organically, slowly coaxing a disjointed structure into something personal and profound.

Their approach defies contemporary renovation culture's obsession with swift reveals. By working within financial and seasonal constraints, they created space for thoughtful decision-making that honors both the barn's agricultural bones and their own sensibilities. The result challenges rural living conventions through strategic modernization; floor-to-ceiling windows, for example, dissolve traditional boundaries while respecting the building's original silhouette.

North Barn is also distinguished by its curatorial sophistication. Working with a local antiques dealer, Craig and North created interiors that layer Moroccan textiles, mid-century furniture, and Hudson Valley–specific materials into something that feels both worldly and rooted to place.

The barn now functions as both a private retreat and a community gathering place—where Sunday roasts flow seamlessly into garden conversations and seasonal celebrations. Through energy-efficient additions, modern comfort supports rather than compromises historical integrity. At North Barn, patience becomes a design principle, proving that the most meaningful transformations can't be rushed, but rather carefully cultivated over time.

Opposite The traditional barn is situated on a sprawling plot of land in the Hudson Valley of New York, surrounded by uninterrupted forestland, rolling hills, and low mountains.
Above The owners, who renovated and expanded the barn over a 14-year period, embraced an English country cottage aesthetic but employed modern architectural gestures to let in more light.

Opposite A furry friend cozies up next to the generous working fireplace, which is flanked by a comfortable reading chair and a vibrant antique rug. *Above* During the renovation, the owners reimagined the floor plan for better flow, more light, and to adapt each room into a warm, lived-in space. Here, a view of the staircase that connects the lower living areas to more intimate spaces on the upper floor.

Opposite The seasonal rhythms of nature heavily influenced the design, as seen in this bathroom adorned with nods to local flowers.
Above Whether dining al fresco or retreating into bedrooms layered with
curated textiles and furnishings, the owners use the barn both as a social gathering space and a private escape.

Right In the new extension, spacious windows add a modern sensibility to an otherwise traditional barn silhouette.

PLANTOPEDIA

Glenbeigh, County Kerry, Ireland

When Ruins Become Refuge

There's something almost too perfect about a cottage that was literally lost before being rediscovered. But Lost Cottage's story resists romanticism through the kind of stubborn devotion that turns a goat shelter back into a superb human habitation over a span of 10 long years.

After two decades in Paris, the owner's return to Ireland in order to tackle this ruin suggests something more complex than nostalgia. This is architecture as futurist archaeology, peeling back layers to discover not what was, but what could be. The owner's decision to source larch wood from the surrounding forest, and to employ traditional lime-rendering specialists, reveals an understanding that authentic restoration is more about continuation than replication.

The result feels inevitably right, with minimalist interiors that breathe with the landscape rather than compete against it. The poured-concrete extension, with its wood-grain oxidized surface echoing the surrounding mountain colors, shows how contemporary intervention can honor historic fabric. It's a sophisticated response to place, one that avoids overly precious preservation and thoughtless modernization.

The glass-roofed bathroom, where guests can bathe under Ireland's first International Dark Sky Reserve, captures the project's essence: luxury redefined as an intimate connection to nature's elements. This isn't an escape from the world but a more intentional way of inhabiting it, proving that some of the most meaningful refuges sometimes require long journeys—both temporal and geographical.

Opposite From above, the red roof of Lost Cottage stands out amid the wild greens and blue lake of the storied Kerry landscape.
Above Inside, soft green textiles, hand-troweled plaster walls,
and a cool stone floor create a grounded sanctuary that feels both contemporary and timeless.

Above A robust stone hearth anchors one of the bedrooms, while salvaged and vintage pieces add layers of warmth.
Opposite Earthy materials, gentle light, and pared-back design define the open kitchen and living spaces.

The Concert Hall

Some houses accumulate stories naturally while others are built precisely for them. Dragonfly, which sits on 130 acres (52.6 hectares) in Hillsdale, upstate New York, serves both approaches: here one finds careful restoration work, which recognized good bones beneath years of neglect, alongside an acoustically perfect main room constructed for intimate concerts.

The property's previous incarnation reads like a cultural footnote: a musician's retreat where a grand piano anchored performances that became coveted invitations among Hudson Valley cognoscenti. That legacy lives on in the room's proportions and acoustic qualities, even as the space has evolved. The restoration that followed honored this musical heritage while adapting the sprawling, 7,200-square-foot (670-square-meter) home for contemporary rural living.

What emerges is a rare synthesis of European grandeur and Hudson Valley pastoral sensibility. The estate's setting takes full advantage of the landscape: a deep lake with a smaller counterpart beyond; rolling terrain perfect for cross-country skiing; and multiple fireplaces that encourage cozy, post-activity gatherings. The balance between connection (20 minutes to Hudson and the Berkshires) and secluded sanctuary reflects a sophisticated understanding of countryside living.

This is cottagecore scaled up without losing intimacy, as the property shows how grand gestures can serve humble pleasures, and where concert-hall acoustics now amplify conversations and the everyday rituals of rural retreat.

Opposite Originally built by a pianist seeking an acoustically perfect home for intimate concerts, the living space and bedrooms spotlight sweeping proportions.
Above The property sits on 130 acres (52.6 ha) of a sprawling estate—including multiple lakes and rolling hills—in upstate New York.

This is cottagecore scaled up without losing intimacy, as the property shows how grand gestures can serve humble pleasures.

Above The interiors merge European elegance with a rural, Hudson Valley sensibility, as seen in a hallway accented with a medley of artworks and a bathroom with a woven stool and industrial-style black finishes.
Opposite Despite the home's impressive size, at 7,200 square feet (670 m^2), each room feels like an intimate sanctuary that encourages inhabits to experience the best of country living.

Darlinghurst, Sydney,
NSW, Australia
by Studio PULP

A Stable Story

Above The exterior of the converted stable shows the original sandstone construction surrounded by courtyard walls, with its distinctive pitched roof maintaining the authentic character that the architects chose to honor rather than overwrite. *Opposite* Inside, natural materials dominate, with preserved sandstone walls and exposed wooden beams throughout.

Tucked into a hidden lane in Darlinghurst, this former horse stable has been reimagined as a layered, personal urban sanctuary. Rather than overwriting its history, the design honors it by embracing sandstone walls, timber beams, and weathered floors as collaborators rather than constraints.

Inside, the approach subverts cottage clichés: raw textures meet contemporary contrasts. Vibrant artworks, sculptural lighting, and bursts of color play against the tactile warmth of stone, creating a space that feels both nostalgic and current. Upstairs, a loft—once used to store hay—offers a tranquil retreat. Soft grays, creamy whites, and natural fibers craft a calm haven, while wooden barn doors open to reveal a leafy courtyard below, letting light and city breezes inside.

Outside, a lush garden unfolds, transforming daily rituals into slow, sensory experiences. Bi-folding doors blur the boundary between interior and nature, turning the small footprint into a generous, flowing space.

Every detail, from refined wooden staircases to gentle uplighting, merges history with modern ease. The result is a cottage that doesn't mimic a romantic rural past but celebrates character, warmth, and unexpected joy. It invites you to live alongside its story rather than merely inhabit it.

Opposite A living area celebrates the contrast between the raw sandstone walls and modern furnishings in vibrant pops of color. *Above* Living and dining areas prioritize warmth and comfort through curated furnishings and a seamless connection to the outdoors via large doors, transforming the small footprint into a generous, flowing space.

Red Hill, Brisbane, Australia
by zuzana&nicholas architects

The New Vernacular

114 Red Hill House and Studio

When architects Zuzana Kovar and Nicholas Skepper acquired this 1910 Queenslander worker's cottage in Brisbane's Red Hill, they confronted a century of renovations that had stripped away the building's material integrity. Rather than attempt a faithful restoration, they embraced radical pragmatism, transforming the compromised space into a contemporary interpretation that houses both their family and work life.

The solution challenges suburban conventions by reviving the mixed-use typology of historic shophouses. The architecture studio occupies the lower level, the veranda shielded from the street by steel mesh screens. Above, domestic spaces unfold amidst the cottage's original wood-frame construction, yet feel decidedly contemporary.

What distinguishes this project is intelligent adaptation: by containing all functions within the original footprint, the architects preserved green space while creating a semi-external quality that's rare in cottage interiors. Large sliding doors dissolve boundaries between inside and out, and enable natural ventilation for much of the subtropical year.

The result shows how historical structures can accommodate radically different ways of living without sacrificing character. Here, work and domesticity coexist through careful zoning: clients access the studio independently via a side street, while children occasionally claim the workspace as an extra play area. This fluid boundary between public and private, professional and personal, suggests new possibilities for cottage life beyond the typical romantic retreat.

Opposite The dining room opens generously to the garden beyond, blurring the line between indoors and out. Sleek glass panels invite nature into daily rituals.
Above The home's original form was preserved, with new windows and materials echoing the Australian landscape.

Opposite An airy upper level connects different zones with a minimal steel balustrade and open shelving.
Above A thoughtful palette of wood, stone, and concrete creates interiors that feel both intimate and expansive.

The fluid boundary between public and private, professional and personal, suggests new possibilities for cottage life beyond the typical romantic retreat.

Above Rich wood floors ground the kitchen and a bedroom.
Opposite A cocoon-like corner lounge in caramel-toned leather and wood offers a relaxing place to pause.

Tisbury, Massachusetts, USA
by Maryann Thompson Architects
and Mother Studio

The Gathering House

Above The home's "pinwheel" configuration allows daylight to enter rooms from multiple sides of each wing, which were purposely kept long and thin.
Opposite Architect Maryann Thompson, as well as the home's owners, intended for the home to be woven into and enhance the natural beauty of its idyllic surroundings in rural Massachusetts.

When a restaurant chef and his wife build a country home, expect the kitchen to hold court. At Suppertime, Maryann Thompson's pinwheel configuration places her clients' culinary passion at the center of everything—a decision that reflects both professional instinct and domestic wisdom. This isn't vernacular architecture trying to be modern: it's modern architecture fluent in vernacular.

Thompson's gabled wings suggest a house assembled over generations, yet the interior spaces flow with ease. Large panels of glass replace traditional punched windows, flooding rooms with light while maintaining the familiar New England silhouette. The architect's most inspired move might have been the positioning of skylights on both sides of the gable ridge beam, washing the exposed roof structure in light, "just as," the architect notes, "the sun washes tree branches in the landscape."

Materials speak to place without resorting to pastiche. Salvaged-wood floors celebrate knots and imperfections, while hand-glazed kitchen tiles catch ambient light. The exterior's cedar shingles and shiplap will eventually weather to gray, achieving what Thompson calls an "almost fabric-like quality." Most striking are the round cedar porch columns, milled on a massive wood lathe using techniques rooted in the shipbuilding traditions of Martha's Vineyard.

For the owners, Suppertime represents rural living reimagined in the spirit of hospitality. Interior windows connect the kitchen to other spaces while maintaining acoustic separation, and outdoor courtyards provide overflow for gatherings. This is architecture that posits the radical notion that country homes should enhance, not inhibit, the art of bringing people together.

This isn't vernacular architecture trying to be modern: it's modern architecture fluent in vernacular.

Above In a nod to New England vernacular, the walls are clad in salvaged wood marked by knots and other minor aesthetic imperfections.
Opposite With a spacious table and upholstered benches lining the room,
the dining area allows the owners (one of whom is a professional chef) to entertain and host gatherings of any size and type.

Beyond Nostalgia

How a New Generation Redefines Rural Architecture.

This new vernacular emerges from a generation of architects that understands the difference between copying and learning.

In the hands of 21st-century architects, vernacular forms have shed their nostalgic fetters. Where once gabled roofs and wood frames signaled a retreat into pastoral fantasy, they now represent something more urgent: a gradual return to architectural styles anchored in place, material, and restraint. This is the new vernacular, not an imitation of the past so much as a reinterpretation through contemporary sensibility.

On Torö Island in Sweden, for example, James Hamilton and Malin Heyman's renovation of a 1970s catalog house (page 138) exemplifies this shift. Rather than concealing structural necessities, they exposed ridge beams and columns to serve as defining features, celebrating structural honesty over cosmetic perfection. Their material prudence—think tar paper nodding to the original dark exteriors, or pine plywood complementing existing paneling—reflects the values of homeowners who prioritize authenticity over fleeting trends.

This approach extends across countries. Over on Germany's Baltic coast, Jan Henrik Jansen and Marshall Blecher's restoration of a 120-year-old crofter's cottage (page 22) demonstrates vernacular reinterpretation through thoughtful restraint. They left the street-facing facade deliberately untouched—a subtle tribute to the regional vernacular—while contemporary interventions emerge gradually, with a black-steel dormer providing the first clue of transformation within.

Such projects often resist the picturesque. Craig Hutchinson's Maker's Barn (page 172) in the English countryside challenges the traditional compartmentalization often seen in rural dwellings, offering spatial fluidity within a 700-square-foot (65-square-meter) space that was once an abandoned agricultural building. Clay-plastered walls, end-grain parquet flooring, and local elm borrow colors and texture from the surrounding landscape while reinterpreting local architectural language for modern tastes.

This new vernacular emerges from a generation of architects that understands the difference between copying and learning. Whereas previous rural

Opposite A bedroom featuring sleek lines, natural materials, and abundant light at this home on Töro Island in Sweden demonstrates how contemporary architects celebrate structural honesty over cosmetic perfection.
Above In a hallway, hints of the past—from the wooden floor and ceiling to the plaster walls—mingle with a calming color palette and contemporary furniture, exemplifying the new vernacular's approach of learning from tradition rather than copying it.

Above A living area opens to surrounding fields through sweeping glass windows, showing how modern cottagecore homes create dialogue with nature through transparency and contextual sensitivity rather than nostalgic retreat. *Opposite* Heather's House in Australia demonstrates the "new vernacular" principle of building in harmony with place, where the architecture breathes with its surroundings.

revivals often trafficked in theme-park-style domesticity, today's architects treat vernacular traditions as living languages rather than museum pieces. They recognize that the stereotypical gabled forms and wood frames evolved from practical necessities (climate, local materials, construction methods) rather than aesthetic whims.

At its most sophisticated, the cottagecore movement embodies this nuanced understanding of place. It's not about recreating an imagined past and more about recovering principles of building that industrial construction abandoned: economy of means, contextual sensitivity, and what might be called rural intelligence. This intelligence manifests in Duncan Greenaway's glass intervention (page 156) at a 15th-century thatched cottage in Farleigh Hungerford, England, where transparency preserves heritage via contrast rather than mimicry.

The result is an architecture that breathes with its surroundings rather than standing apart—spaces that appear, as Craig Hutchinson notes, "as if they were always there," while subtly revolutionizing expectations of rural living. This new vernacular suggests that the most radical act in contemporary architecture might be one of the oldest ones: building in harmony with place.

Right Modern extensions thoughtfully integrate with historic structures, as seen in Nieby Crofter's Cottage in Germany, where traditional brick and a thatched roof meet a carefully considered contemporary addition.

Torö Island, Nynäshamn Municipality, Sweden
by James Hamilton and Malin Heyman

Reimagining a Prefab Legacy

On Torö Island, James Hamilton and Malin Heyman's renovation of a 1970s catalog house responds to a general shift in Swedish country living: that of embracing the overlooked instead of starting anew. Housing a grandmother, her daughter and partner, and the couple's small children, this multi-generational getaway embodies a contemporary domesticity that prioritizes communal experience over isolation, adapting modernist efficiency to the needs of today's family.

The architects' approach honors imperfection as a hallmark of character. Worn components are not hidden but pragmatically addressed: damaged roof sections cut back rather than replaced, and structural necessities reimagined as defining features. In exposing the ridge beam, as well as columns where spaces converge, they celebrate structural honesty over cosmetic perfection.

For a family seeking escape from city living, the house offers a marked departure: spaces that balance intimacy with solitude, interiors that respond to landscape rather than imposing upon it. The material restraint (tar paper echoing the original dark exteriors, pine plywood complementing existing paneling) reflects an attitude valuing authenticity over trends.

Torö's modest intervention counters traditional countryside aesthetics by suggesting that meaningful rural dwellings might not be picturesque new builds, but thoughtfully recast existing structures—homes whose character is achieved by respectful adaptation rather than idealized design. It's a quiet manifesto for seeing the potential in what already exists.

Opposite Echoing the dark brown-black ferrous pigment of the original facades, the architects chose to paint the extension exterior in a brown-black tar paint, as seen here from the northern property edge.
Above A renovated fireplace, built-in bench, and a new post-and-lintel roof structure breathe new life into the living room.

Right The home is nestled within a dense forest canopy on Torö Island, where the deep connection with nature allows this multi-generational retreat to offer a different pace from city living.

Above Pine plywood was used throughout the home's interior, from living spaces and the kitchen to intimate study nooks.
Opposite A cozy bedroom looks out onto the garden.

Captain Kelly's Cottage

Bruny Island, Tasmania, Australia
by Wardle

Weathered Wisdom

In a remote bay on Bruny Island, where the Southern Ocean meets the coastline's pastoral sheep farms, Captain Kelly's Cottage stands as a thoughtful counterpoint to our culture of constant renewal. Painstakingly restored by Wardle, the 1840s weatherboard dwelling offers a contemplative alternative to the accelerated rhythms of mainland Australian life.

Originally built by a maritime adventurer during whaling offseasons, the cottage had endured decades of misguided alterations prior to its careful resurrection. Rather than concealing the structure's age, Wardle's approach celebrates it: they exposed newspaper clippings that once insulated its walls, as well as aged wood and brick infill, letting the cottage's fascinating, storied past speak for itself.

A new living area now bridges the two original structures (the bedrooms and kitchen), while the elements of the veranda—namely its layered soffit and exposed ceiling rafters—extend throughout, binding old and new in a cohesive architectural narrative.

The cottage functions as a refuge, where mainland urgencies dissolve into the rhythms of the weather and tides. Remade spaces accommodate modern comfort without sacrificing character, creating an environment where distraction yields to the present moment.

Via its weathered boards and thoughtfully revealed construction techniques, Captain Kelly's Cottage encapsulates something increasingly rare: an architecture that measures time not in trending aesthetics but in generations of human experience.

Above An 1840s-era cottage originally constructed by a maritime adventurer, Captain Kelly's Cottage sits on a rugged and remote sheep farm on Bruny Island, Tasmania.

Opposite Historical materials, such as aged wooden beams and brick infill, are celebrated rather than hidden in the home's kitchen/dining area.

Opposite Great craftsmanship—a challenge given Bruny Island's remote location—is displayed throughout the renovation, as seen in the woodwork of this contemporary room.
Above Intended to be used as a refuge for relaxation, the home's pared-back yet warm sensibility can be felt from the exterior through to the interiors.

Opposite The wide veranda was an important source of inspiration for the renovation, as it effectively unites the new spaces added onto original structures.
Above From dining spaces to bedrooms, the home echoes the stories and history behind its first inhabitants in the 19th century.

Right The cottage enjoys sweeping views of the surrounding rugged hills and waterfront—the perfect environment for a slower, more considered way of living.

Farleigh Hungerford,
Bath, United Kingdom
by Duncan Greenaway,
Greenaway Architecture

Transparency as Preservation

In Farleigh Hungerford, a 15th-century thatched cottage posed a delicate question to modern countryside living: must heritage always imply darkness, energy inefficiency, and disconnection from the surrounding landscape? Duncan Greenaway's elegant response is a glass intervention that transforms the stone cottage's relationship with place while also maintaining its character.

With its thin frames and glass-to-glass corners, the pavilion performs a remarkable act of preservation through contrast. By clearly delineating new from old, it allows the original structure's story to remain visible while reframing the dwelling's relationship with the adjacent watercress pond and spring, a relationship that once made the northwest wall so unbearably cold.

Materials reveal intention: natural stone flooring and exposed wood echo the cottage's rustic palette, while ultra-thin glass acts as an efficient counterpoint to the centuries-old masonry. The sedum roof further blurs boundaries between structure and landscape.

For the family of four within, this intervention altered their experience of rural living. Whereas the cottage once offered mere glimpses of nature through small apertures, it now provides panoramic immersion. The space has become warmer, more communal, and more efficient, shifting daily rituals away from adaptations to the historic structure and toward genuine engagement with both heritage and landscape. This is countryside living reimagined, not through the rejection of history but through complementary contrast—where modern transparency preserves rather than erases.

Opposite Attached to a 15th-century thatched cottage, the contemporary glass extension complements the existing structure by adding more flow, light, functionality, and a feeling of space.
Above The floor-to-ceiling glass allows the owners to now enjoy views of the surrounding nature, including an adjacent watercress pond and a nearby spring.

Birregurra, Victoria, Australia
by Gardiner Architects

Rooted in the Land

On the sweeping edge of Barwon Valley in Birregurra, this sustainable farmhouse stands as a graceful testament to a new kind of rural living where environmental stewardship and intergenerational connection thrive side by side. Designed with a sensitivity to the region, this off-grid sanctuary balances modern comfort with a respect for the land's rhythms and resilience.

The owner's vision for her family is woven into every detail: a place where children and grandchildren gather, where flexible spaces adapt to visiting guests, and where the act of living is intertwined with nurturing the earth. The design is pragmatic yet poetic, oriented to shelter from harsh winds while embracing sweeping vistas. A courtyard is a perfect space for tranquil mornings, while over 2,500 native plantings restore eroded land, fostering biodiversity and reviving the farm's ecological vitality.

Crafted from locally sourced lumber and prefabricated mass-timber structures, the house celebrates resource efficiency without sacrificing warmth or beauty. Solar panels, a wood-fired boiler, and a sophisticated transpiration septic system power a truly off-grid lifestyle, offering the inhabitants both independence and intimacy with nature.

This is a home that breathes and evolves, a place where food is grown, rainwater is harvested, and every season is felt. The farmhouse embodies a future-forward rural ideal: adaptable, nurturing, and profoundly connected to the landscape.

Opposite With a neutral color palette and furnishings that reflect the rural setting, a living area features expansive windows that frame sweeping views of the Barwon Valley landscape, creating a seamless connection between the graceful interiors and the native plantings that foster biodiversity across the property.
Above The home sits within the rolling farmland of Birregurra, Victoria, where over 2,500 native plantings help restore eroded land. The house's orientation provides shelter from harsh winds yet embraces the panoramic vistas.

This sustainable farmhouse stands as a graceful testament to a new kind of rural living where environmental stewardship and intergenerational connection thrive side by side.

Above A kitchen and bedroom showcase the sleek modern architecture, with natural wood-paneled ceilings that celebrate resource efficiency while maintaining the warmth essential to this gathering place. *Opposite* The home embodies true sustainability through its off-grid systems, which include solar panels, a wood-fired boiler, and a sophisticated transpiration septic system—allowing for complete independence while nurturing the land's ecological vitality.

Loch Ness,
Scottish Highlands,
United Kingdom
by Ruth Kramer

Scandi Meets Scot

Above With touches of Highland heritage mixed with signature Nordic restraint, the interiors exude what designer Ruth Kramer calls "Scandi-Scot" style.
Opposite The traditional stone dwelling dates to the 19th century, and its historic character was brought back to life through a series of thoughtful interventions.

This former manse overlooking Loch Ness presents a compelling case for cultural cross-pollination. What Swiss designer Ruth Kramer calls "Scandi-Scot" style emerges as more than a trend; it's a deliberate marriage of Highland heritage with signature Nordic restraint, one that sidesteps both tartan cliché and cold minimalism.

The 19th-century stone dwelling had previously been stripped of its character by several modernizations, leaving Kramer and the owners to excavate authenticity from beneath decades of misguided updates. Their approach was methodical and resourceful: oak flooring salvaged from nearby Aldourie Castle replaced synthetic carpeting, while four-poster beds sourced from the same estate were thoughtfully brought back to life by local joiners. Half the new furnishings arrived second-hand, earning their place in the home through thoughtful refurbishment.

The resurrection of practical elements—think cornices recast from original molds and fireplaces that were uncovered and restored—suggests a particular kind of domesticity. At Tigh na Coille, the past serves present needs without the burden of nostalgia. Hans Wegner's Papa Bear chair stakes a corner by the fire not as a flashy design statement but as a refuge for reading, embodying the house's insistence that comfort and culture need not compete. The result feels at once rooted and worldly, showing that thoughtful stewardship can honor place while embracing broader inspirations.

Opposite An iconic Papa Bear chair by Hans Wegner encourages cozy relaxation in a corner of the home. *Above* Practical elements, such as fireplaces, were carefully uncovered and restored, while newer additions—including a spacious bathtub—nod to the past.

Outer London, United Kingdom
by Craig Hutchinson, HUTCH

Deconstructing Cottage Boundaries

In the English countryside near Petworth, Craig Hutchinson's transformation of a derelict agricultural building challenges rural living's traditional compartmentalization. Whereas most cottage renovations might seek to impose rigid divisions between spaces, the Maker's Barn embraces fluidity as a 700-square-foot (65-square-meter) retreat separated not by walls but by thoughtful interventions.

The central concrete fireplace acts as an anchor, with strategically placed openings offering glimpses between living and sleeping areas. Built-in cabinetry helps shape the layout while keeping it open. Even the sunken bathtub offers a view of rolling hills—a conscious rejection of the typical countryside retreat's inward focus.

This approach reflects a shift in how we consider heritage spaces. Rather than replicating the surrounding Tudor vernacular, Hutchinson reinterprets local architectural language for contemporary sensibilities.

Materials blur boundaries between inside and out, with clay-plastered walls, end-grain parquet flooring, and local elm, each borrowing hues from the surrounding landscape. The furnishings, from Mario Bellini's Camaleonda sofa to handmade ceramics and wooden objects, extend the architecture's dialogue between craftsmanship and context.

The result is a countryside dwelling that breathes concurrently with its surroundings rather than standing apart—a space that appears, in Hutchinson's words, "as if it was always there," while subtly revolutionizing expectations of rural living.

Opposite The exterior of the Maker's Barn. For the architects, it was essential for the renovated structure to harmoniously blend into its surroundings.
Above A central board-framed concrete chimney anchors the space, dividing up the living/kitchen areas on one end of the cottage and the bedroom/bathroom spaces on the other.

Materials blur boundaries between inside and out, with clay-plastered walls, end-grain parquet flooring, and local elm, each borrowing hues from the surrounding landscape.

Above The materials used throughout—clay-plastered walls and ceilings, end-grain parquet flooring, and English elm wood millwork—all reflect the tones of the surrounding English countryside.
Opposite The high-level kitchen rack was purposely positioned to retain spectacular views from the kitchen island.

Opposite Subtle changes of level were incorporated throughout, including this sunken bath, so that the owners could live and experience the space and its views differently.
Above The architects designed the renovation so that spectacular vistas of the surrounding landscape could be enjoyed from every position and point of the building, as seen here in a bedroom and living space.

Hécourt, Normandy, France
by Emmanuel Guilloux and
Clément Mathieu, Studio Guma

A Quiet Dialogue Between Past and Present

At Maison Hécourt, rural life is neither romanticized nor remade; rather, it is subtly rebalanced. In the hands of Studio Guma, this 19th-century farmhouse in Normandy becomes a study in continuity, where the agricultural past lingers not through aesthetics but through structure and mood. Architects Emmanuel Guilloux and Clément Mathieu envisioned the home as a sanctuary, as a place to slow down and reconnect without retreating into nostalgia.

Their approach honors the site's dueling histories: a former cart shed now serves as a spacious kitchen and dining space open to the garden on two sides, while the old stable plays host to a living room. Each building retains its spatial identity, yet together they form a coherent and fluid domestic landscape.

Modest material interventions—steel, concrete, and lacquered aluminum—thread through the original stone and wood, adding durability without displacing character. The result is a rural home that resists the picturesque, offering simplicity without the cliché. At the *maison*, daily life aligns with the surrounding landscape's rhythms: morning light streams into the kitchen, while sunsets invite residents to the terrace.

This is rural living reframed as a lived practice of restraint, resourcefulness, and quiet renewal. Maison Hécourt suggests that today's country living can be less about escape and more about recalibration, where imperfection is embraced as character and modernity comes through via pared-back alterations.

Opposite Connection to the outdoors—through sliding doors, windows, and garden access—reinforces an ongoing relationship between the house and the surrounding nature. Here, a small dining patio sits adjacent to the kitchen. *Above* Original timber-and-stone walls nod to the home's rural past.

Each building retains its spatial identity, yet together they form a coherent and fluid domestic landscape.

Above Originally a main farmhouse and two agricultural outbuildings, the architects decided to maintain the different special identities—open, narrow, dark, and tall—in their modern adaptation.
Opposite A spacious, double-height room that opens to both sides of the garden, the kitchen is housed in what was once the former cart shed.

Shelter Island, New York, USA
by Workstead

Evolving a Coastal Legacy

186 Shelter Island House

In an age of architectural spectacle, Shelter Island House emerges as a compelling counter-narrative, where humility and thoughtful restraint serve as the foundations for a more intentional relationship with place. Workstead's expansion of this 1940s cottage demonstrates how architectural lineage can be honored while subtly evolving to meet contemporary needs.

The project's most eloquent gesture is the glass-walled breezeway connecting the original structure to a new bedroom pavilion, creating a U-shaped plan that cradles a south-facing courtyard. This transitional space serves as both a physical connector and a philosophical statement: a transparent threshold between past and present that frames the landscape while making the passage of time tangible within the home's daily rhythms.

Rather than erasing history, Workstead's approach reveals layers of habitation through measured interventions: cedar shingles unify old and new volumes while nodding to the island's 19th-century vernacular; cathedral ceilings and gable forms have been carefully preserved; and white oak flooring provides a natural counterpoint to the original tile. By removing the central chimney, they introduced a new source of light and spatial movement. Finally, reconfiguring the bathroom allowed the kitchen to expand into a more communal locus for family life.

For the clients, the home's modest elegance represents an alternative vision of rural luxury: one defined not by scale or ostentation but by tactile materiality, considered proportions, and spaces that promote a deeper awareness of seasonal change and natural light.

Above A perfect expression of the home's balance between intimacy and openness, a soaking tub in the primary bathroom frames beautiful garden views.
Opposite Exterior details like cedar shingles and gabled forms create continuity with the past, while interior features such as exposed beams and a robust stone hearth ground the space in rustic warmth.

Above Details reveal the home's subtle luxury and material honesty: a kitchen washed in light, a pool, a stone sink, and a narrow window that slices a hallway with shifting sunbeams.

Opposite A striking, red artwork animates a hallway, set against blue stone tiles and timber beams above in an interplay of color and texture.

Western Sjælland, Denmark
by Jan Henrik Jansen
and Marshall Blecher

Vejrhøj's Second Chapter

Above The new interiors echo Danish architect Ole Meyer's original design from 1967.
Opposite The renovation maintained the thatched roof and exposed wooden construction, which Meyer employed as an homage to traditional farmhouses of the surrounding area.

When architects uncover traces of what might have been, the past often extends an invitation. Such was the case with Ole Meyer's iconic 1967 Vejrhøj summerhouse, a once-celebrated expression of Danish vernacular. The original structure stood as a quiet manifesto: traditional thatched roofing above exposed wood and minimal sliding windows—a modernist interpretation of the regional farmhouse typology.

By 2018, the architectural gem faced erasure after decades of neglect and evolving building codes. Architects Jan Henrik Jansen and Marshall Blecher approached its restoration with reverence, essentially rebuilding the structure while honoring its conceptual integrity. Contemporary demands required inventive updates: custom composite columns with steel cores sheathed in pitch pine allowed for slim window profiles, while high-performance insulation now hides beneath floorboards and behind millwork.

Perhaps most compelling was their discovery of Meyer's unrealized vision for a second volume. This became the blueprint for a concrete counterpoint to the wooden original, housing guest quarters and utility spaces while shaping a dramatic new entry sequence. Visitors now approach via a sunken path, passing beneath the thatched eaves and through the new structure to arrive in a wind-sheltered courtyard bridging old and new.

The six-year restoration transcends preservation: it's a dialogue across decades, where contemporary interventions respond in harmony to Meyer's original vocabulary. Vejrhøj breathes again.

The original structure stood as a quiet manifesto: a modernist interpretation of the regional farmhouse typology.

Above The apparent simplicity and minimalist aesthetic of the modern restoration belies intricate craftsmanship and technical feats that took six years to complete.
Opposite This landmark of Danish architectural heritage is nestled in the rolling hills of western Sjaelland.

Eltham, Australia
by Michael R. Young

A Cinematic Sanctuary

Tucked within the bushland of Eltham, a suburb of Melbourne, this mudbrick cottage feels like a scene from a storybook—a retreat where creative energy and rural tranquility intertwine. Originally crafted in 2001 by mudbrick designer Michael R. Young, the two-bedroom haven captures the spirit of the region's artisan architecture, echoing the earthy elegance of Alistair Knox and Robert Boyle.

Stepping past the rustic red front door, you're welcomed into an intimate world of exposed wood-beam ceilings, mudbrick walls, and red-brick floors that exude a grounded charm. Floor-to-ceiling windows dissolve the boundary between inside and out, framing the surrounding treescape like living paintings.

Though the owner, a cinematographer, spends much of his year traveling for film projects, this modest sanctuary offers him a rare stillness. Here, life slows with the comforting crackle of the Oblica fireplace or casual evenings with friends on the front porch. The interiors, an evolving mix of Scandinavian and Japanese influences alongside eclectic finds, remain faithful to the home's earthy essence while adding personal touches.

A cottage of this scale feels delightfully manageable yet profoundly soulful, a cocoon where its owner can fully recharge between cinematic ventures. Eltham Cottage embodies a deeply personal rhythm of life: quiet, creative, and harmoniously connected to nature.

Opposite An open living and dining area features exposed wooden beams overhead, terra-cotta tile flooring, and a central Oblica fireplace surrounded by plush furnishings—creating an intimate, grounded atmosphere.
Above A sitting area opens directly onto the garden through floor-to-ceiling windows that dissolve the boundary between inside and out, framing the surrounding Eltham bushland.

The interiors, an evolving mix of Scandinavian and Japanese influences alongside eclectic finds, remain faithful to the home's earthy essence while adding personal touches.

Above Two corners of the home showcase the wood-paneled walls and ceiling used throughout, demonstrating how Michael R. Young's mudbrick design creates a cohesive sanctuary where natural materials establish an earthy elegance.

Opposite A cozy bedroom achieves perfect balance between intimacy and light, with the warm wood ceiling overhead providing cocoon-like comfort while the side window maintains the home's connection to the surrounding treescape.

Novato, Marin County, California, USA
by Peter Dolkas of Studio Dorion
and Fergus Garber Architects

Building in Good Company

Peter Dolkas faced a delicate proposal: to build a new construction on a 1920s Marin County farm that wouldn't upstage the original farmhouse where his brother's family had settled. His solution sidesteps competition through what he calls "sibling" architecture, honoring familial DNA while asserting independence.

The challenge proved as much psychological as architectural. Where his family expected paint colors and wallpaper selections, Dolkas committed to Douglas fir paneling on walls, ceilings ... everything. This all-wood envelope creates what he describes as an interior glow, establishing warmth without ornament. Reclaimed heart-pine flooring, sourced from a South Carolina barn, adds a patina that new constructions often lack.

The wraparound porch doubles the living space, capitalizing on Northern California's temperate climate and blurring indoor-outdoor boundaries. More significantly, the structure orients itself around a mature oak tree visible from the kitchen and living areas—a memorial to Dolkas's maternal grandfather.

Modern amenities hide in plain sight: a refrigerator and freezer disappear behind matching wood panels; surround-sound speakers are invisibly integrated; and air conditioning operates sight unseen. This technological stealth allows contemporary comfort while preserving the structure's agrarian sensibility. The finished space accommodates both daily life and multigenerational gatherings—evidence that thoughtful new construction can honor both place and family harmony.

Opposite This new construction nods to the history and heritage of the 1920s-era Marin County farmland upon which it sits.
Above Reclaimed heart-pine flooring sourced from an old barn in
South Carolina complements the Douglas fir paneling to bring warmth and patina to this dining area.

Opposite Though the house exudes a rugged, agrarian sensibility, modern comforts, such as speakers and air-conditioning, were thoughtfully integrated and hidden in plain sight. *Above* Historically used throughout homes in Northern California, Douglas fir paneling envelops everything in the house, from dining spaces and bedrooms to bathrooms.

Right Large windows allow natural light to pour into the open living and dining area, creating the perfect setting for the multigenerational family gatherings that define this home's purpose.

Camber, East Sussex,
United Kingdom
by Marta Nowicka

Essential Lookout

Above The dining area (top) centers around a magnificent 500-year-old medieval dining table, bathed in natural light from overhead skylights, while the pared-back palette of neutral tones creates a calming atmosphere that lets the cottage's utilitarian origins shine. *Opposite* The kitchen extension serves as the home's social center, with panoramic windows framing views across the distinctive landscape toward Dungeness.

Interior architect Marta Nowicka's approach to this derelict coastguard cottage near Camber Sands reveals something vital about contemporary rural living: authenticity often emerges from understanding the logic of the past rather than merely mimicking it. Where others might have imposed quaint cottage fantasies onto this structure, Nowicka excavated the building's utilitarian DNA—thick walls that protect against strong seaside winds, and robust proportions favoring function over ornament.

The transformation unfolded over several years, a deliberate slowness that allowed the structure to dictate its own evolution. Vandalized interiors became opportunities for material honesty. Exposed plaster replaces wallpaper; salvaged floorboards carry their original scars; and a medieval dining table anchors a kitchen extension that feels more like a maritime workshop than a country hearth. Steel surfaces and rope handrails acknowledge the sea's proximity without coastal cliché.

This isn't preservation as a museum piece, but rather as a living document—a former urban dweller's astute recognition that, sometimes, rural authenticity lies in adaptation rather than imitation. The cottage's stripped-back interiors remove distraction, thus creating space for contemplation that follows the surrounding tidal rhythms rather than urban schedules. Here, imperfection becomes character, and restraint reveals essence.

Opposite An upstairs bedroom showcases the cottage's authentic character with exposed ceiling beams, whitewashed walls, and generous skylights that flood the space with coastal light.
Above The exterior features a garden constructed from reclaimed materials, creating a protected threshold between the cottage's minimalism and the coastal environment, while the interior's stripped-back aesthetic allows the dramatic seascape and sky to take center stage through windows.

Plener Istebna

Istebna, Silesian Beskids, Poland
by Justyna Boduch and Mistovia

Mountain Heritage Meets Modern Retreat

At the convergence of the Polish, Czech, and Slovak borders, two wooden cottages perch on a hillside, emblematic of a growing desire to slow down and reconnect with place. Plener Istebna taps into the cottagecore ethos by merging regional vernacular with contemporary comfort and authenticity. What began as a simple structure evolved into twin structures: here, thoughtful material choices and vintage curation forge spaces that feel both rooted and refreshed.

Plener Istebna is the brainchild of two friends—Tomek, an athlete raised in the mountains, and Miłosz, a city-dweller with deep family ties to the region. Working in collaboration with architect Justyna Boduch and interior-design studio Mistovia, the pair saw their vision come to life. The 754-square-foot (70-square-meter) cottages, nicknamed "Stone" and "Terracotta," share the same layout but diverge: "Stone" balances wood and bright neutrals atop a graphite floor mimicking Calacatta marble, while "Terracotta" exudes a warm, earthy narrative through tile and corduroy.

Mistovia's vintage-forward approach augments the spirit of slowness, rejecting fast furnishings in favor of timeless pieces. Czech design features prominently, including a TV stand from František Jirák and Tatra Nábytok pieces from the 1960s.

The interiors avoid clichés often seen in contemporary retreats, connecting to place without employing pastiche. Decorative ceramics and clay-plaster walls evoke tradition while framing, rather than contending with, the sweeping mountain views. These are spaces to dwell in, not merely escape to.

Above Not far from the Polish-Czech-Slovak border, this vacation cottage sits on the rolling hills in the heart of the Silesian Beskids. *Opposite* In the living room, abundant plywood, neutral nature-inspired hues, and a dark graphite floor all contribute to a warm, relaxing atmosphere.

MIŁOSZEWSKI

Above Scandinavian furnishings, Czech design, natural materials, and hints of regional architecture of the Silesian Beskids make for a space that feels vintage and thoroughly modern all at once.
Opposite A rust-hued chair brings a sense of modern vibrancy to the neutral palette of materials in a corner of the cottage.

Pound Ridge, New York, USA
by Rafe Churchill and Brad Ford

Material Memory

226 Barnegat Barns

Lizzie and James Hammel's thoughtful barn conversion demonstrates that sustainability and sophistication need not be mutually exclusive—a lesson that feels particularly relevant for urban refugees seeking rural authenticity without sacrificing discernment.

What began as a Covid-19 pandemic refuge evolved into something more permanent: a meditation on materials that connects Manhattan's industrial past to Westchester County's agricultural heritage. Heart-pine floors salvaged from a 1890s warehouse near New York City's High Line now anchor rooms where 1850s barn bones have been stripped to their essential proportions. This isn't nostalgic preservation but material archaeology, with each reclaimed element carrying forward its own narrative while thoroughly serving contemporary needs.

The Hammels, reclaimed-wood specialists and founders of the Hudson Company, approach restoration with professional reverence for wood's inherent qualities. Original hayloft floors find new purpose, and ash trees felled by invasive beetles become sculptural wood stacks. Their kitchen features baskets by contemporary craftsman Jonathan Kline, nodding to the town of Pound Ridge's 19th-century basketmaking tradition but avoiding museum-like preciousness.

The result challenges rural living's false choice between utility and beauty. Children freely play among exquisite antiques, while a French wine screw from the 1850s coexists alongside modern family housewares. This is country living for urbanites who refuse to check their aesthetic sensibilities at the gate.

Opposite The exterior showcases the authentic character of the original 1850s structure in Pound Ridge, New York, where weathered siding and traditional roofing materials are framed by a timeless rural setting.
Above Inside, exposed wooden beams overhead define the converted barn's architecture, while reclaimed materials and a light, airy palette bridge the home's agricultural past with its modern rural lifestyle.

The Art of Making Do

How Cottagecore's Embrace of Repair and Reuse Challenges Contemporary Consumption.

The perfectly curated home gives way to the thoughtfully accumulated one. Beauty emerges from care rather than capital.

In an era defined by algorithmic abundance and instant acquisition, the cottagecore movement champions a radical alternative, suggesting that satisfaction might emerge not from purchasing, but from preserving; not from accumulating, but from adapting. This ethos of "making do" represents more than aesthetic choices: it marks a fundamental rejection of contemporary consumption culture and its promises of fulfillment through endless renewal.

The practice of salvaging furniture most tangibly embodies this philosophy. Whereas mainstream design culture often promotes coordinated sets and pristine finishes, practitioners of cottagecore embrace the mismatched chairs, the paint-worn table, the cabinet with eclectic hardware and perhaps of questionable provenance. These pieces carry stories that new furniture cannot; they show evidence of previous lives, accumulated patina, and the particular charm that results from decades of use. The act of restoring a piece of furniture represents a kind of meditation, where each hour spent sanding or reupholstering acts as a deliberate counterpoint to the instant gratification of online shopping.

Textile crafts extend this philosophy into intimate daily rituals. Mending clothes, darning socks, and sewing kitchen linens transform necessity into mindful practice. The #visiblemending movement on social media celebrates imperfection as decoration, transforming rips and stains into opportunities for creative interventions. It recalls the traditional Japanese stitching technique known as *sashiko,* where visible garment repairs serve both decorative and functional purposes. That a mended object could become even more beautiful in its repaired state is a direct challenge to throwaway culture's preference for perfect replacements.

The secondhand sourcing that defines many cottagecore interiors reflects broader cultural shifts toward conscious consumption. Driven by climate anxiety and economic uncertainty, younger generations increasingly view thrift stores and estate sales not as last resorts, but as go-to treasure troves.

Opposite This corner of the home showcases the thoughtful mishmash that defines cottagecore interiors: ceramics, patterns, a lamp, paintings, a chair, table, and a colorful rug come together in an embrace of the imperfect and eclectic.
Above A gold frame and flower arrangement rest on a mantelpiece, demonstrating how cottagecore finds beauty in the accumulated rather than the acquired.

Above A traditional brick home with a thatched roof embodies the countryside idyll that cottagecore seeks to preserve—structures that have weathered decades through repair and adaptation rather than replacement.

Opposite A wooden table and chairs occupy a shaded outdoor spot, representing the movement's preference for furniture that bears the patina of use.

The transformation of secondhand shopping from stigmatized necessity to cultural statement parallels the movement's broader rehabilitation of rural life. The chipped ceramic pitcher, the hand-knitted throw, the slightly worn cookbook … these objects gain value precisely through their imperfections and associations.

This embrace of repair and reuse finds fertile ground in social media's anti-consumption corners, where users document decades-old wardrobes and celebrate furniture that's inherited rather than purchased. These accounts offer critiques of lifestyle content's relentless newness and, in turn, suggest alternative measures of domestic success. The perfectly curated home gives way to one that evolves organically over time. Beauty emerges from care rather than capital.

Ultimately, the cottagecore commitment to thrift and craft represents something more profound than aesthetic preference or economic necessity. It suggests a reimagining of domestic life itself, where pleasure derives from process rather than product; where imperfection itself becomes a design principle; and where the act of "making do" becomes a form of cultural resistance. In hands that mend rather than discard, objects accumulate meaning that no algorithm or fleeting trend can replicate.

LLOYD'S
SIGNAL STATION

Left A maritime cottage perched high on the Cornish cliffs, built in 1872, stands as a testament to the philosophy of making do. It's a structure that's endured the rugged coastal environment through careful maintenance and thoughtful adaptation.

Veliko Tarnovo Region,
Bulgaria
by Tim Clinch

Liberation Through Color

This Bulgarian cottage renovation represents something radical in contemporary rural living: the deliberate rejection of taste in favor of joy, and a professional photographer's rebellion against decades of "good" interior design.

Weary of magazine-perfect interiors, photographer Tim Clinch found refuge in Bulgaria's cheap property market. What began as economic necessity evolved into aesthetic liberation. The cottage, purchased for the price of a decent car, became a laboratory for unlearning habits. Where his camera had once captured endless variations of beige and faded French furniture, his home embraces red against green walls—a color combination that breaks every rule of refined taste.

This isn't rustic chic; it's purposeful anti-chic. Rough, original wood-framed windows remain; handmade tiles replace modern alternatives; and cheerful clutter supplants curated minimalism. Clinch distributed quotidian items across multiple buildings—linens stored in the barn, books housed separately—forcing daily movement through the property. The strategy, learned from French designer Frédéric Méchiche, transforms domestic routine into an active engagement with space.

The home challenges cottagecore's occasional tendency toward nostalgic perfection. Clinch's approach suggests that rural living might require abandoning urban aesthetics entirely, embracing instead what locals consider beautiful, rather than what magazines deem tasteful. His cottage proves that joy makes for the most livable spaces.

Opposite The exterior overlooks the picturesque village near Veliko Tarnovo, Bulgaria, with plantings that complement the traditional architecture.
Above A bedroom features cheerful decor found in local antique shops and flea markets, while the painted green ceiling adds to the joyful atmosphere that defines this cottage.

Opposite The kitchen embraces a vibrant green and red color scheme with traditional stone flooring, creating a cozy space that prioritizes cheerfulness over conventional "good taste."
Above A charming dining nook continues the home's green and red palette, while traditional Bulgarian sleeping alcoves built into the walls with handcrafted wooden frames are surrounded by colorful textiles.

GET
WELL

Lovett Bay, Sydney, Australia
by Richard Unsworth

Where Time Bends with the Tide

Accessible via the waters of Lovett Bay, Richard Unsworth's Trincomalee reveals a counter-intuitive approach to the rural retreat: embracing a structure's accumulated contradictions instead of erasing its eccentric history. Originally built in 1896 and reworked in the 1980s, this waterside cottage isn't particularly concerned with aesthetic unity.

The main house remains structurally untouched, with its rare Australian hardwood left unpainted. Unsworth's intervention emerges instead through careful curation: mid-century furniture, textiles, and artifacts introduce color and texture. The once-weathered caretaker's cottage, updated in 2024, now functions as a contemporary complement while retaining its own historical elements, including an uncovered cobbled fireplace. Unsworth's approach challenges the frequent impulse to impose uniformity on older spaces. Rather than perfection, Trincomalee offers authenticity—layered, occasionally contradictory, and inherently unique.

The home's relationship with setting—a grove of endangered spotted gum trees—defines everything. A decade-long garden restoration saw invasive species removed and native plants restored, while the central outdoor space serves as a threshold between architecture and the outdoors.

For its inhabitants, Trincomalee demands a different relationship with daily life. Boat-only access means shedding urban rhythms at the shore. Here, priorities shift toward what Unsworth calls "melting into the surrounding bush," where modernity becomes secondary to beauty, and connection to place becomes a kind of luxury.

Opposite Throughout the interior, rare Australian hardwood was purposely left unpainted.
Above Nestled in a grove of spotted gum trees, the cottage is only accessible via water at Lovett Bay.

Opposite A view of the exterior of the home and its lush surroundings. The property reflects a mix of styles and centuries, as it was originally constructed in 1896 and updated in the 1980s.
Above The smaller caretaker's cottage, which was completely renovated in 2024, boasts its own sense of style and modernity. Inside, an original cobbled fireplace was uncovered.

Opposite Owner Richard Unsworth relaxing in a light-filled room enlivened by a collection of plants. For him, the home's connection to nature was the guiding principle throughout his thoughtful restoration.
Above Reflecting the eclectic spirit of the home, most of the interior furnishings are French, Danish, African, or Moroccan antiques and flea market finds discovered during the owner's travels.

Fawley Bottom, Henley-on-Thames, Oxfordshire, United Kingdom

Artful Subversion of a Rural Idyll

Above Timber frames and overhead beams are present throughout the interiors, nodding to the home's Georgian heritage.
Opposite Originally constructed in the 18th century, the wood-frame structure was originally employed as a bakehouse to supply bread to the surrounding villages and farmland.

In the hamlet of Fawley Bottom, this heritage-protected former bakehouse exposes the false binary between preservation and reinvention. With its symmetrical Georgian facade, this four-bedroom cottage finds expression in the tension between architectural purity and modernization.

The original wood-framed structure, dating to the early 18th century, remains visible with exposed beams overhead and wall panels throughout. However, these elements now frame spaces reimagined with a distinctly modern sensibility. The plaster infill is painted in vibrant hues rather than period-appropriate whitewash; the kitchen balances cozy proportions with strategically placed skylights; and a bathroom's colorful tiling deviates from rural renovations' typical palette of neutrals.

Most revealing is how the cottage reflects changing patterns of contemporary pastoral life. The garage (a 20th-century necessity) has been repurposed into an office and workshop, accommodating remote workers who have relocated to rural settings. The garden balances aesthetics and practicality, with herb plantings positioned conveniently near the kitchen.

This approach reflects a growing sophistication in countryside living, one that rejects both urban transplantation and nostalgic fantasy. Despite its proximity to London, this home isn't a mere weekend escape. Instead, it's an expression of contemporary rural domesticity: history-conscious without being history-bound, secluded without being isolated, and characterized by creative integration instead of compromise.

Above Pops of color and eclectic design objects and furniture—including a treehouse-like bed in a child's bedroom—bring a sense of modernity to the historic home.
Opposite Complete with a low garden wall and flower and herb beds, an adjacent patio area invites outdoor entertaining.

BOVRIL
CORNED BEEF

The Stones

Clydesdale, Central Victoria, Australia

The Long Game

Above Kiwi fruit vines climb over the pergola beside the old milking sheds, softening their agricultural past with a romantic touch.
Opposite Once the site of early morning milkings, the corrugated iron sheds are now fully sealed and transformed into guest quarters.

Jeremy Valentine and Grant Francis, the vintage dealers behind Melbourne's Shag stores, have spent over a decade proving that city sophistication and rural ambition need not be mutually exclusive. Their 16-acre (6.5-hectare) estate in central Victoria unfolds as a master class in patient curation, with five buildings dating from the 1850s to 1920s, each assigned a distinct personality through strategic restraint.

The main stone house, beautifully restored by the previous owners, grounds the collection in English countryside gravitas. Here, Victorian-era finds and cottage-kitchen pragmatism establish domestic hierarchy. The rehabilitated stone barn, meanwhile, leans more modern, with mid-century treasures and contemporary collections freed from period constraints. Even the 1920s milking sheds earn contemporary purpose as guest quarters "intentionally lost in time."

The duo's disciplined eclecticism extends to the sprawling garden, where trial and error trumps professional landscaping. Mediterranean stalwarts—olives, lavender, and rosemary—stand alongside cold-climate cacti and robust euphorbias, forging microclimates that honor Victoria's extreme seasons. This approach reinforces something deeper than simple hobby farming—it's a recognition that authentic rural living demands both romantic vision and pragmatic adaptation. Twelve years in, with sheep paddocks established and projects guided by "what the place tells us," the Stones estate demonstrates how former urbanites might honor historic bones while avoiding heritage's theme-park tendencies.

Above Vintage ceramics, rambling gardens, and a lovingly restored kitchen define the Stones' mix of old-world charm and playful individuality. Each space feels deeply personal and was curated over time.
Opposite A weathered antique table, chairs, and a 1920s green cabinet ground the dining area in rustic warmth.

Opposite In the milking sheds' alcove bedroom, vivid linens meet an antique wooden chest, celebrating the owners' love of layering eras in every corner.
Above From garden plantings to interior living spaces, the Stones estate mirrors its owners' colorful, eclectic eye.

Arnarstapi, Iceland
by Baulhus,
Hálfdan Lárus Pedersen

The Merchant's House

Above The living room and kitchen honor the house's 18th-century origins with reclaimed wood floors, aged stone, and exposed timber beams overhead.
Opposite This historic merchant house sits dramatically on a rugged coastline, with its weathered exterior facing the Atlantic Ocean as it has since 1770.

Perched on Iceland's dramatic Arnarstapi cliffs, this meticulously restored 17th-century merchant's house embodies rural living's deepest aspirations: it rejects aesthetic performance in favor of authentic communion with place and time. Architect Hálfdan Lárus Pedersen's intervention transcends conventional restoration, instead orchestrating a dialogue between weathered bones and contemporary needs.

The project's genius lies in its subtractive approach, its removal of modern impositions to reveal the house's inherent beauty. Reclaimed wood, aged stone, and traditional Icelandic wool create a material palette that breathes history. Local crafts—from bespoke hardware to hand-painted bird motifs—weave regional traditions into the narrative.

Crucially, the house maintains its original orientation toward the Atlantic, honoring the sea-facing stance that once welcomed merchant vessels. This gesture anchors the home to the rhythms of the landscape rather than those of contemporary convention.

Here, cottagecore's romantic ideal finds its most sophisticated expression through the patient cultivation of belonging. The home's tight quarters demand custom solutions, with each piece of furniture thoughtfully integrated so as to maximize both function and character. The resulting sanctuary encourages slowness, fosters presence, and demonstrates that authentic rural living emerges from a deeper engagement with place.

Above The interiors embrace rawness and simplicity, with dark reclaimed wood dominating the walls, while furnishings crafted by local Icelandic artisans and vintage textiles woven from traditional Icelandic wool create layers of texture and warmth. *Opposite* The intimate dining nook features custom-built banquette seating upholstered in handwoven fabrics, surrounded by wood paneling adorned with paintings of local bird species—an artistic touch that brings the abundant wildlife of the surrounding cliffs indoors.

Styal, Cheshire, United Kingdom
by Annabelle & Co.

Organic Evolution

Above Interiors mix historic and contemporary elements, with original exposed cruck timber beams providing dramatic overhead structure while modern finishes create an airy, light-filled space.
Opposite The new oak-framed glasshouse extension creates an indoor-outdoor living space, where vines climb overhead and abundant natural light floods through the glass ceiling, bridging the 17th-century cottage with contemporary life.

Authentic rural renovation often results from habitation and its process of discovery, as evidenced by this 17th-century dowager cottage by Annabelle Russell.

The cottage's history almost reads like architectural archaeology: an original cruck frame, a Tudor-era facade, and a roof that was later raised by a resident accustomed to grander proportions. Russell found the property rain-soaked and bucket-riddled, but beneath the damp and dated finishes lay extraordinary craftsmanship. Her approach avoided the typical heritage trap, instead treating the building as a living document requiring contemporary translation.

The transformation unfolded organically as Russell's family inhabited the space, which allowed daily life to inform decisions. A problematic 1990s extension became an opportunity: oak framing now creates a window transition between the cottage and garden, while contemporary interventions, such as the plywood breakfast booth, frame historic beams without competing. Padded linen walls offer contemporary comfort within ancient proportions, and reclaimed materials maintain continuity across the centuries.

Russell's professional expertise in vernacular architecture informed every decision, from restoring original windows to exposing hidden wooden frames. Norcliffe Grange challenges rural living's false choice between historic preservation and modern comfort, as it shows that respectful adaptation can honor the past while embracing the present.

Opposite The home's original proportions are celebrated on the upper level, which showcases the building's authentic vernacular architecture while serving modern living needs.
Above The exterior reveals the thoughtful renovation approach, while inside, the bespoke plywood breakfast booth nestled beneath historic beams creates an intimate dining space that perfectly captures the home's dialogue between past and present.

Mérey, l'Eure, Normandy, France
by Céline Boclaud

Riverside Reverie

Above A living room and bedroom showcase the original materials that the architect chose to preserve and celebrate—stone walls and exposed beams overhead in the living room, and a pitched roof with wooden beams in the bedroom—demonstrating how the renovation embraced the home's rustic spirit.
Opposite An outdoor terrace sits next to the Eure River in Normandy, spotlighting the home's profound relationship with nature.

In the quiet village of Mérey, along the banks of the Eure River, Céline Boclaud has transformed a traditional country house into a contemporary refuge. The renovation focused on harmonizing old and new—optimizing space by converting the attic into a bright office and turning an old workshop into a warm, inviting room.

Rather than erasing the home's rustic soul, Boclaud embraced it: original stone walls, lime-painted surfaces, and waxed concrete floors ground the house in timeless elegance. In the master bedroom, warm lime-washed walls and shell-shaped sconces create a cocoon-like atmosphere that feels personal and soothing. Throughout the interiors, handcrafted decor and natural materials evoke a sense of artisanal charm without slipping into cliché.

Large windows in the attic now frame sweeping views of the river, turning workdays into moments of connection with the landscape. Downstairs, the kitchen overlooks the water, making daily cooking feel like floating on a boat when the river rises. A small terrace on the riverbank has become the center for summer mornings, where breakfasts unfold alongside birds drifting by.

With thoughtful updates that respect tradition while inviting in light and warmth, this riverside cottage redefines country living as both intimate and endlessly inspiring.

Index

Marin County Farmhouse
USA
pp. 206–213
Photography: Ethan Herrington/ethanherrington.com
Architect: Fergus Garber Architects
Designer: Peter Dolkas of Studio Dorion

Mount Stapafell Cottage
Iceland
pp. 268–275
Photography: Mikael Lundblad
Architect: Hálfdan Lárus Pedersen/Baulhus/baulhus.com

Nieby Crofter's Cottage
Germany
pp. 22–27
Photography: Jose Campos/josecamposphotographer.com
Architects: Jan Henrik Jansen Arkitekter/janhenrikjansen.dk & Studio Marshall Blecher/marshallblecher.com

Norcliffe Grange
United Kingdom
pp. 276–281
Photography: courtesy of The Modern House/themodernhouse.com
Architect: Annabelle & Co

North Barn
USA
pp. 86–95
Photography: Gabriel Zimmer/Catskill Image/catskill-image.com

Old Bakehouse
United Kingdom
pp. 254–259
Photography: Paul Whitbread for Inigo/inigo.com

Plener Istebna
Poland
pp. 220–225
Photography: ONI studio/@onistories
Interior Design: Mistovia/@mistovia

Red Hill House and Studio
Australia
pp. 114–121
Photography: Clinton Weaver/clinton-weaver.com
Architect: zuzana&nicholas architects/zuzanaandnicholas.com
Builder: Thirdson Constructions

Riverside House
France
pp. 282–285
Photography: Bertrand Fompeyrine/BCDF Studio

Shelter Island House
USA
pp. 186–193
Photography: Matthew Williams
Architect: Workstead/workstead.com
Styling: Mike Ten Have

Suppertime
USA
pp. 122–129
Photography: Jeremy Bitterman Photography
Architects: Maryann Thompson Architects/maryannthompson.com
Interior Designer: Mother Studio
Landscape Architect: Michael Van Valkenburgh Associates Inc

Sydney Horse Stable
Australia
pp. 108–113
Photography: Alisha Gore/The Design Files
Styling: Jono Fleming
Architects: Studio PULP

The Maker's Barn
United Kingdom
pp. 172–179
Photography: Helen Cathcart/helencathcart.com
Architect & Interior Design: HUTCH/hutchdesign.co
Styling: HUTCH & Sarah Birks
Joinery Construction: Jacob Alexander
Contractor: AK Construction

The Signal Station
United Kingdom
pp. 42–47
Photography: Unique Homestays/uniquehomestays.com

The Stones
Australia
pp. 260–267
Caitlin Mills/The Design Files
Styling: Annie Portelli

Tigh Na Coille
United Kingdom
pp. 166–171
Photography: Fran Mart/franmart.co

Torö
Sweden
pp. 138–145
Photography: Andy Liffner
Architects: Atelier–Heyman Hamilton/at-hh.com
Styling: Matsson Marnell
Contractor: Lynn bygg AB

Trincomalee
Australia
pp. 246–253
Photography: Nicholas Watt *(pp. 251, 252, 253 bottom)* and Anson Smart *(pp. 246–250, 253 top)*/@trinco.pittwater

Vejrhøj Summerhouse
Denmark
pp. 194–199
Photography: Agatzke
Architects: Jan Henrik Jansen Arkitekter/janhenrikjansen.dk & Studio Marshall Blecher/marshallblecher.com

Cottagecore

New Countryside Living

This book was conceived, edited, and designed by gestalten.

Edited by Iris Hempelmann and François Luc-Giraldeau
Research by Effie Efthymiadi

Written by Victorine Lamothe

Editorial management by Arndt Jasper and Anna Diekmann

Design, layout, and cover design by Hy-Ran Kilian

Image curation by Madeline Dudley-Yates

Cover image by Helen Cathcart / helencathcart.com
and HUTCH / hutchdesign.co
Back cover image by Mikael Olsson / mikaelolsson.se
in collaboration with MAGNIBERG bed wear
at Carl and Karin Larsson House / magniberg.com

Production management by Martin Bretschneider

Typefaces by KOMETA Typefaces (Victor Serif)
and François Rappo (Plain)

Printed by optimal media GmbH, Röbel/Müritz
Made in Germany

Published by gestalten, Berlin 2025
ISBN 978-3-96704-192-7
1st printing, 2025

For more information and to order books, please visit www.gestalten.com

Die Gestalten Verlag GmbH & Co. KG
Mariannenstrasse 9–10
10999 Berlin, Germany
hello@gestalten.com

Bibliographic information published by the Deutsche Nationalbibliothek
The Deutsche Nationalbibliothek lists this publication in the Deutsche Nationalbibliografie; detailed bibliographic data is available online at www.dnb.de

None of the content in this book was published in exchange for payment by commercial parties or designers; gestalten selected all included work solely on the basis of its artistic merit.

This book was printed on paper certified according to the standards of the FSC®.

FSC www.fsc.org MIX Paper | Supporting responsible forestry FSC® C108521